ACROSS

AND

DOWN

The ABC's of Solving
Crossword Puzzles

By

Adrienne M. Cadik

TABLE OF CONTENTS

ABOUT THIS BOOK

"Across and Down" is for people who enjoy solving crossword puzzles and who want to enhance their experience by increasing their puzzle-solving skills.

For some readers, the information presented here may be common sense concepts that you already know. But seeing the tips and techniques organized in black-and-white for the first time may be surprisingly helpful.

A large vocabulary and an encyclopedic memory of facts are always great assets, but they are not necessary for puzzle-solving. More important are an inquiring mind, a natural curiosity, and a willingness to think outside the proverbial box.

Anyone who appreciates intellectual challenges and the beauty of language can experience enjoyment and satisfaction from solving crossword puzzles. This book presents strategies and tips for approaching the crossword puzzle as a whole and through its individual clues. The goal is, in a word, fun.

WHAT'S IN IT FOR YOU

You'll get a great mental workout. Solving puzzles enhances many brain activities: spatial perception, flexible thinking, pattern recognition, creativity, information retrieval, and memory.

You'll have fun. As the tips in this book help you become a better solver, your level of enjoyment will increase. A good puzzle is full of witty clues and clever answers.

You'll expand your store of knowledge. You'll learn about geography, popular culture, current and historical events, science, and literature.

You'll enhance your skills. Your vocabulary, spelling ability, and feel for the English language will improve.

You'll experience real satisfaction. There's that great "aha" feeling after you've risen to a challenge, struggled, and mastered it.

This guide will help you improve your skill at solving crossword puzzles. As with many games, you'll have more fun as you become better at it.

Come join the millions of people who enjoy and appreciate this incredibly popular indoor sport.

GENERAL
GUIDELINES

THE RULES FOR SOLVING CROSSWORD PUZZLES

THE RULES: There are no rules. Enjoy it your way.

COROLLARY #1: Use whatever reference materials you need. Solving crossword puzzles is a learning experience, so go ahead, look up words and facts, and learn as much as you can. You aren't "cheating" because there's no cheating in a game with no rules.

COROLLARY #2: Use whatever media you prefer. Do it the traditional way on paper, using a pencil, an erasable pen (recommended), a non-erasable pen, or a crayon (not recommended). Or do it online, using one of the many puzzle websites.

COROLLARY #3: Solve the clues in whatever way makes it the most fun. The guidelines in this book describe techniques that will improve your solving efficiency. If a different technique works better for you, go for it. Enjoyment trumps efficiency.

EXCEPTION TO THE NO-RULES RULE: If you're doing your puzzle as part of a competition, then there are rules (of course). To add a new dimension to your puzzle-solving, consider entering one of the online competitions or local tournaments.

TERMINOLOGY and BASICS

The entire physical **puzzle** – its pattern of **symmetrical** black and white **squares** - is called the **grid**.

You are the **solver.** The person who develops the grid and decides what should go into the white squares is the **constructor**. The constructor and/or **editor** writes instructions so that the solver can fill all those white squares correctly.

The definitions, hints, and phrases that direct the solver to complete the puzzle are the **clues**. The solution to a clue is an **answer**, also called an **entry** when it refers to what you put into the white squares of the grid. Entries that go into the grid from left to right are "**across**" answers, and they correspond to Across clues. Likewise, "**down**" entries go from top to bottom and correspond to Down clues.

Many puzzles have a **theme,** where related clues apply to several entries, usually the longest ones. All entries that are not related to the theme entries are called **fill**.

Most American puzzles are square, with a symmetric pattern of black and white squares. All squares are checked (i.e., clued both across and down). There are no islands (unconnected sections). Answers are at least 3 squares long.

GO EASY ON YOURSELF

Puzzle with a friend.

Take a break when you get stuck. Come back later. The cobwebs may have cleared.

Don't make arbitrary rules or demands on yourself. The "right" way is whatever is most satisfying for you.

Practice with puzzles in the style you like best. If you get to know the constructors and editors whose puzzles you most enjoy, you can look for collections of their work or publications that carry them.

Improve by cross-checking your answers when you're done. See what you missed and remember it for next time.

Choose the level of difficulty that is appropriate for you. You want to be challenged but not tortured. The difficulty level is usually a function of:

- The ratio of black squares to white. If there are fewer black squares, and thus big chunks of white squares, the puzzle will be harder.

- The trickiness of the cluing.

- The day of the week. In many daily publications, the puzzles get harder through the week.

GETTING STARTED

Scan the set of clues for a "gimme", a clue that can have only one possible answer. Fill-in-the-blank clues stand out easily. Names of well-known people, places, and titles may also catch your eye and be good starting places.

Scan for clues that suggest a common grammatical or spelling pattern, such as a prefix or suffix. These will be covered in more detail under Specific Tips.

Start with clues that lead to short answers of 3 or 4 letters. These are usually the easiest, and there are many common repeaters. You'll make good use of answers like ERA, AREA, ARIA, ORE, EASE, ALE, ATE, IRE, and LEI.

Don't start by guessing the answer to an ambiguous clue. Wait until you've already entered a few letters.

If there's a title or theme, let it guide you.

USE WHAT YOU ALREADY KNOW

Go for answers where there are already some letters. In fact, work a whole interlocking area at a time. Taking advantage of the pattern of crossing answers is your most useful strategy.

Letters you've already entered that are at the beginning of a crossing word are the most useful. For example, an E or S provides a more helpful hint if it's the first letter of a word rather than the last.

Take advantage of any uncommon crossing letters that you've entered, such as J, K, Q, V, W, X, or Z. They provide a good hint for the crossing word.

Trust your skills in English. You can recognize which letter patterns are common or uncommon at different positions in a word. For example, you might be skeptical of NG being at the beginning of a word but know it's a normal pattern to be at the end. Look for reasonable vowel/consonant combinations.

When stumped, you can always resort to testing each letter of the alphabet in an empty square.

Keep a "Crossword Crib Sheet", a list of obscure words, abbreviations, and expressions that frequently appear as answers in crossword puzzles. Add to it often, and refer to it when you're solving.

EXPECT THE UNEXPECTED

Watch for clues that are ambiguous or tricky. The meaning, form, or pronunciation may not be the most obvious one. For example, which meaning would you select for the answer (5 letters) to a clue like "Set"? STAGE, as in "movie set"? GROUP, as in "a set of objects"? FIXED, as in "set in stone"? You need a few helpful crossing letters before deciding on your answer.

Remember that answers can be multi-word phrases, titles, and names. Also, be aware that the adjacent letters where the words meet may look very odd. For example, the clue "Request" might yield the multi-word phrase "ask for", written in the puzzle as "ASKFOR". The "SKF" in the middle of the answer looks alarmingly incorrect until you realize the letters are parts of two different words.

Expect answers that include something other than normal words. Puzzles may contain special characters, numbers, words entered backwards, etc. Some puzzles have a rebus element, where multiple letters are entered in a square.

Pay attention to your grammar. Clue and answer should be interchangeable. Though the clue may be tricky and ambiguous, it will always agree with the answer in grammatical form. For example, if the clue is a plural noun, the answer will be a plural noun; if the clue is a past-tense verb, the answer will be a past-tense verb.

Be especially alert when there's a question mark at the end of the clue. It indicates a tricky answer, such as a pun or other play on words.

Expect at least some "crosswordese". To accommodate odd letter crossings, constructors are often forced to include entries that are obscure, dreadfully overused, or grammatically questionable. These are usually short, vowel-heavy words that are used more often in crosswords than in everyday English. They are bricks onto which constructors can lay more interesting fill.

Don't assume that every answer you've already entered is correct. Be prepared to crosscheck for reasonable alternatives.

CLUE APPRECIATION

Take time to appreciate the talent and thought that goes into constructing a good clue. The quality of a crossword puzzle is largely a function of the quality of its clues.

A clue must provide enough information to allow it to be solved, but in a very small amount of space, at an appropriate level of difficulty, and preferably with wit and challenge. Many of them are little gems.

Read each clue with every possible interpretation, usage, and pronunciation. Practice creative parsing. Watch for misdirection, ambiguity, and wordplay. Keep an open mind.

Features marked "Clue Appreciation" will appear under several of the Specific Tips. Each will demonstrate a well-constructed clue, with an explanation of how to interpret and solve it.

SPECIFIC
TIPS

ABOUT THE TIPS

This section contains many hints for analyzing different types of clues.

Note that there may be several hints that could apply to the same clue. The section "Clue Appreciation" demonstrates some clever clues that could be solved using any of several approaches. Whatever you do to derive the correct answer is right!

The examples associated with the tips will be presented as follows:

EX: Clue => ENTRY

Like all crossword puzzle clues, the clues in these examples will begin with a capital letter. The rest of the clue will be in lower case, except for proper nouns and titles that are normally capitalized. The entry, or answer, will be displayed in capital letters. The arrow ("=>") points from the clue to its answer.

CLUE SHORTHAND CONVENTIONS

To provide all the information that a solver needs in a very short amount of space, the clues use shorthand conventions that indicate the type of answer required.

The following are commonly abbreviated instructions that indicate the form of the answer. They are usually found at the end of the clue, following a colon or in parentheses.

Abbr. Abbreviation

Arch. Archaic

Colloq. Colloquial

Obs. Obsolete

Var. Variant spelling

Sl. Slang

Dial. Dialect

Pref. Prefix

Suf. Suffix

Fr. French

It. Italian

Ger. German

Sp. Spanish

The question mark (?) is a special symbol indicating that the clue contains wordplay.

DEFINITIONS, SYNONYMS, & FACTS

The most common and straightforward clue is a simple **definition, synonym, or fact**.

EX: Angry   => IRATE

     Land measure   => ACRE

     Author of "The Raven"   => POE

     Biggest land mass   => ASIA

If you get stuck in a tricky section of a puzzle, it's these straightforward clues that are easiest to look up. Make use of a website, dictionary, thesaurus, atlas, or whatever. You can get un-stuck in this puzzle and learn something new along the way.

CLUE APPRECIATION

EX: Black-and-white cookie   => OREO

     Dunkable, twistable snack   => OREO

     1912 food invention   => OREO

     Kosher, vegan cookie   => OREO

These are all factual clues at different levels of difficulty, yielding a wildly common crossword answer. (Look at all those vowels!)

EX: Part of a foot => INCH ("foot" is a unit of measure)

=> ARCH ("foot" is a body part)

Note that, even if the crossings have allowed you to enter the letters "CH" in the 3rd and 4th positions of the answer, the 1st and 2nd letters are still ambiguous. With either answer, this is a straightforward factual clue. But it cleverly takes advantage of the multiple meanings of "foot" and of the coincidence of the letter pattern in those two possible answers.

FILL IN THE BLANKS

Most crossword puzzles will have at least a few clues that are fill-in-the-blank types, also called **partials**. The answer may be one or several words.

Single word answer:

EX: Mai ____ => TAI

____-Cat => SNO

Fleur de ____ => LIS

No place like ____ => HOME

Multi-word answer:

EX: From ____ to Z => ATO

____ broke => GOFOR

PAIRINGS

A **pairing** clue is looking for a common partner word.

EX: Partner of neither	=> NOR
Egg go-with	=> HAM
Precedes luck or waiter	=> DUMB
Something to lend or bend	=> ANEAR ('an ear')

SINGULARS AND PLURALS

If the clue indicates a **plural noun**, the answer must be a plural. Likewise, a singular clue yields a **singular noun** answer.

The clue can be a straightforward plural itself, or it may contain hinting words like "and" or "et al."

EX: Big parties   => GALAS

Navy, pinto, et al.   => BEANS

Martin and Charlie   => SHEENS

Your likeliest plural answer will have an 'S' at the end. Play the odds and try an 'S'. But be on the lookout for answers with irregularly spelled plurals.

EX: Honkers   => GEESE

Usage of "or", "for one", and "for example", usually indicates a **singular** answer.

EX: Soprano, for one   => TONY

Dead or Red   => SEA

GRAMMAR ALERT: Watch for clues that can be interpreted as either singular or plural.

EX: Craft   => BOAT or BOATS

School members   => FISH or FISHES

SUFFIXES & PREFIXES

If the clue indicates a person who does some **action**, try 'ER' at the end of the verb to make the noun.

EX: Bakery specialist   => ICER

If the clue indicates a **comparative or superlative**, try 'ER' or 'EST' at the end. If it indicates the **negation** of an adjective, try 'UN' in front.

EX: More like a pin   => NEATER

   Maximally bright   => SMARTEST

   Not right   => UNTRUE

If the clue asks for a description of **how** something is done, try the adverb ending 'LY'.

EX: Way to be disputed   => HOTLY

CLUE APPRECIATION

EX: Faster   => DIETER

Here, the word "faster" is someone who isn't eating, not a comparative adjective for "speedier".

EX: Butter   => GOAT

This "butter" is one who butts, not a bread spread.

EX: Early summer   => ABACUS

This "summer" is not the season, but something that does sums (additions).

VERB FORMS

A **third-person singular** verb is one where the subject is a singular noun or pronoun. The verb usually has an 'S' at the end. Watch for multi-word answers where the 'S' would be in the middle.

EX: Has the flu   => AILS (normal)

   Ails   => HASTHEFLU
    (multi-word)

If the clue is a **past tense** verb, try 'ED' at the end of the answer. Irregular verbs would be exceptions.

EX: Speechified   => ORATED
(normal)

   Opted   => CHOSE
   (irregular)

If the clue indicates a **repeated** action, try 'RE' at the beginning of the answer.

EX: Employ again   => REHIRE

If the clue indicates an **undoing or negating** of an action, try 'UN' at the beginning of the answer.

EX: Remove a knot   => UNTIE

If a clue indicates **being or doing like** someone/something, look for a verb associated with them/it.

EX: Emulate Edison   => INVENT

Remember that past tense verbs may hide as adjectives. (English Major alert! That's a participle.)

EX: Preferred => FAVORITE

Many verbs can be <u>either</u> present or past tense.

EX: Put => PLACE <u>or</u> PLACED

Other examples are SET, HIT, BEAT.

FOREIGN WORDS

If the answer to a clue is a **foreign** word or phrase, the clue will indicate this. The clue can explicitly state the language (using a standard abbreviation at the end of the clue), or it can imply the language via other words.

EXPLICIT: First month (Sp.) => ENERO

IMPLICIT: Calendario page => ENERO

EXPLICIT: State: Fr. => ETAT

IMPLICIT: Pierre's state => ETAT

EXPLICIT: One more than two: It. => TRE

IMPLICIT: One over due => TRE

EXPLICIT: No: Ger. => NEIN

IMPLICIT: Berlin refusal => NEIN

Also, watch for a hint that the answer will have British spelling, as in REALISE or COLOUR.

CLUE APPRECIATION

EX: Crowd in Berlin => DREI

This is a clever play on the expression "Three's a crowd", cluing implicitly that the answer is in German.

EX: Old Italian capital => LIRA

This clue uses an implicit foreign language reference, plus a noun ('capital') with a double meaning.

ABBREVIATIONS AND SHORTENINGS

If the answer to a clue is an **abbreviation or a shortened form** of the full answer, the clue will indicate this.

The clue can explicitly state that the answer is abbreviated, using indicators "Abbr.", "for short", "briefly", "nickname", etc. Or it can imply the answer via an abbreviation or short form embedded in the clue.

EXPLICIT: Airport arrival time: Abbr. => ETA

IMPLICIT: DCA arrival time => ETA

EXPLICIT: Spanish wife title: Abbr. => SRA

IMPLICIT: Mrs. in Madrid => SRA

EXPLICIT: Soviet state: Abbr. => SSR

IMPLICIT: Georgia in 1990, e.g. => SSR

EXPLICIT: Mathematics field, briefly => TRIG

IMPLICIT: Branch of math => TRIG

EXPLICIT: Public servant, for short => POL

IMPLICIT: Dem. or Rep. activist => POL

EXPLICIT: Presidential nickname => ABE

IMPLICIT: "Honest" prez => ABE

SLANG

If the answer to a clue is a **slang** word or phrase, the clue will indicate this.

The clue can explicitly state that the answer contains slang, using indicators "Slang" or "Sl.", "colloquially" or "Colloq.", "informally", etc. Or it can imply the answer via slangy words in the clue.

EXPLICIT: Gangster's girl: Slang   => MOLL

IMPLICIT: Hood's gal   => MOLL

EXPLICIT: Gangster's gun, in slang => GAT

IMPLICIT: Thug's heat   => GAT

EXPLICIT: Beer: Colloq.   => SUDS

IMPLICIT: Brewski   => SUDS

EXPLICIT: Food, informally   => GRUB

IMPLICIT: Chow   => GRUB

GENERAL < == > SPECIFIC

Many clues will provide an example or sub-category of the more **general** answer.

EX: Loafer, for example	=> SHOE
May, say	=> MONTH
Some are spotted	=> OWLS
Yellow or scarlet	=> FEVER

Other clues are general, and they hint that the answer is a **specific** example.

EX: Some ribs	=> PRIME
Kind of estate	=> REAL
One of the signs	=> LEO
A key	=> EFLAT

SOME MORE EMBEDDED HINTS

If the clue indicates someone's **first or last name**, the answer will also be a first or last name, respectively.

EX: Lucy's hubby	=> DESI
Lewis' partner	=> CLARK
Marlon's director	=> ELIA

If the clue is a spoken exclamation or quotation, it will be in quotes, and the answer will also be a spoken word or phrase.

EX: "Woe is me!"	=> ALAS
"Not a chance!"	=> NOWAY
"This could be bad"	=> UHOH

The clue may indicate that the answer is **half or part** of an expression.

EX: Half of an insect	=> TSE (tsetse fly)
Part of a board game	=> TIC, TAC or TOE

The clue may want a **poetic or Biblical** form of a word.

EX: Before, to Keats	=> ERE
Anthem preposition	=> OER

| Biblical ending ('goeth') | => ETH (as in 'goeth') |
| Adam, to Eve | => THOU |

Since a clue and its answer must be grammatically interchangeable, the clue or answer may need to tack on some extra words, usually prepositions.

EX: Seek, with "for" => SEARCH

Must => NEEDSTO

Most American crossword puzzles do not indicate whether the answer contains more than one word or if it is hyphenated. However, some puzzles do specify these situations.

EX: Equal (3 wds.) => ONAPAR

Donkey's call (hyph.) => HEEHAW

CLUE APPRECIATION

EX: Formerly, formerly => ERST

The first "formerly" is a synonym for the answer; the second "formerly" is an embedded hint that the answer is an old-time word.

LETTER PATTERN ANALYSIS

Though spelling in the English language can be maddeningly irregular, you can still make good use of familiar **patterns**. Consider the probability of letters and letter combinations, sequences of consonants and vowels, and of position within an answer.

Some letters are rare as endings:

C, I, J, Q, U, V.

Some letters are usually followed by a vowel when they appear at the start of a word:

H, J, K, L, M, N, Q, R, V, Z

Some letters are strongly suggested in association with other letters:

N before final **G**

G before **HT**

U after **Q**

Some letter combinations are unlikely in certain positions.

> **TR** - OK at the start of a word, not at the end

> **RT** - OK at the end of a word, not at the start

There are letter sequences that indicate a vowel or consonant should be expected.

WH at the beginning of a word is usually followed by a vowel

NK at the end of a word is usually preceded by a vowel

OU in the middle of a word is usually preceded AND followed by consonants

Expect really odd letter combinations in certain circumstances:

- Where words in a multi-word answer meet.

- In abbreviations, where patterns don't apply at all.

- In foreign words, where letter patterns don't follow English spelling rules.

- In the rapidly developing language of texting.

Letters that are common at the ends of words - such as D, E, R, S, T, and Y – will be overrepresented in the bottom row and rightmost column.

SELF-REFERENTIAL (META) CLUES

A **self-referential clue** is one that refers to the actual letters or words within the clue or within the answer.

The clue can indicate a suffix, prefix, or other add-ons for word(s) in the clue.

EX: Land's end   => SCAPE (landscape)

Fire starter   => MIS (misfire)

Verb ending   => OSE (verbose)

Verse opening   => UNI (universe)

The clue can refer to the letters in the words of the clue.

EX: End of fall   => ELS (letters 'L')

Pre-op sequence   => LMN (alphabet series before letters 'OP')

Name in a planner   => ANNE (letters found inside 'planner')

Reversal of fortune backwards)   => HTLAEW ('wealth'

Start of April   => LONGA (long 'A')

Song ender   => HARDG (hard 'G')

The answer may describe words in the clue.

EX: Mice and men   => PLURALS ('mice' and 'men are plural   nouns)

Adjective, e.g.   => NOUN (the word 'adjective' is, indeed, a noun)

Single, for one   => SYNONYM ('single' is a synonym for 'one')

Dash for cash   => TYPO (a typist may enter a 'D' when 'C' is correct)

Ancients, for instance, => ANAGRAM (scramble the letters of 'ancients' and you get 'instance')

CROSSOVER ANSWERS

Answers to clues may **cross over to other clues or answers** in a few different ways.

1. A single clue may direct the solver to continue filling in the answer in multiple places. The answer will typically be a multi-word phrase or title.

EXAMPLE:

10 Across clue: 19th-century author, with 20 Across and 30 Across
=> LOUISA
20 Across clue: See 10 Across
=> MAY
30 Across clue: See 10 Across
=> ALCOTT

2. A clue may refer to the answer of another clue elsewhere in the puzzle.

EXAMPLE, referring to the example in #1 above:

40 Across clue: Novel by 10 Across
=> LITTLEWOMEN
50 Across clue: Character in 40 Across
=> AMY (or Meg, Jo, or Beth)

3. The parts of a long quote or poem may span several answers, indicated by Part 1, 2, etc., or Beginning, Continuation … End.

EXAMPLE:

60 Across clue: Beginning of a humorous poem
=> CANDY IS DANDY BUT

70 Across clue: End of the poem
=> LIQUOR IS QUICKER
(Answers will, of course, not contain those spaces.)

Another EXAMPLE of referring to the answer of another clue:

80 Across clue: Author of 60 Across
=> OGDENNASH (Ogden Nash)

PRONUNCIATION

When reading a clue, remember that words in the clue may have more than one **pronunciation**, and that different pronunciations may indicate different meanings and parts of speech.

EX: Tower	=> something that pulls
Tower	=> a steeple
EX: Flower	=> a blossom
Flower	=> a river
EX: Entrance	=> to charm
Entrance	=> a doorway
EX: Number	=> a numeral
Number	=> an anesthetic
EX: Polish	=> a Slav
Polish	=> to shine
EX: Lead	=> a metal
Lead	=> to guide

AMBIGUOUS CAPITALIZATION

Since **every clue starts with a capital letter**, you can't always be sure whether the first word of the clue is normally a lower-case word OR a proper noun that would normally be capitalized. Many clever clues make use of this ambiguity. The following are all examples where the first word of the clue can serve as both a proper noun and a normal word.

PRODUCT BRANDS

EX: Comet target => SINK ('Comet' is a cleanser)

Time worker => EDITOR ('Time' is a magazine)

Post production => CEREAL

Singer specialty => SEWING

Other popular brands-that-are-also-words include Tide, Dodge, Apple, Gap.

PEOPLE

EX: Tiger's goal => PAR (golfer Woods)

Begin, for example, => ISRAELI (Prime Minister Menachem)

Slaughter in sports => ENOS (baseball player)

Brooks (writer/comedian) => MEL

38

Watch for any word that's also a name, like Bill (Nye), (Lucille) Ball, (George) Bush, (Francis) Bacon.

PLACES

EX: Turkey part   => ANATOLIA ("Turkey" = country)

Mobile home   => ALABAMA ("Mobile" = city)

Superior content   => WATER ("Superior" = lake)

CLUE APPRECIATION

EX: John in England   => LOO

Here, the word "john", a British colloquialism for "toilet", is capitalized only because it is the first word of the clue. The solver is misdirected into thinking of the name "John".

EX: Lab safety org.   => ASPCA

Here, the 'Lab' refers to the Canadian province Labrador and to its namesake retriever dog. The solver is misdirected to think of a science laboratory.

THEMES

Many puzzles have a **theme**, which leads to a consistent topic or pattern throughout. The theme answers will usually appear symmetrically in the grid and in the longest answers.

If the puzzle has a title, the title will provide a hint about the theme. Occasionally, one of the puzzle answers, a "revealer", will provide a hint for the rest of the theme. Some typical themes are:

Numbers

Colors

Foods

Body parts

Sports

Culture: literature, movies, music, fashion

Nature: animals, plants, geographic features

Holidays, often the holiday of the publication date

Quotes, jokes, riddles, or poems, maybe spanning several answers

Wordplay, such as anagrams, palindromes, homophones, malapropisms, heteronyms

Modified spelling, e.g., adding, deleting, or changing letters in the same way across all theme answers

Squares filled with more than one letter (a "rebus") or with non-letters (like pictures, numbers, or symbols)

The main subject of the publication, such as a fishing theme in a periodical about fishing

CLEVER MISDIRECTION

Some clues are **deliberately ambiguous.** i.e., they cleverly lead you to an incorrect first impression of their meaning. The examples below should provide a fair warning not to jump to conclusions when interpreting a clue.

EX: Choose window instead of aisle => ELOPE

Contrary to the first impression, this clue has nothing to do with airplane travel. It refers to climbing out a window instead of walking down an aisle when marrying.

EX: Sign of spring   => ARIES

This "sign" has nothing to do with robins, the equinox, the weather, or flowers. It is one of the astrological signs of spring.

EX: Leaves home   => TEABAG

The answer isn't about running away or moving somewhere, and it is not a third-person verb. It is a noun, the place where tea leaves live.

EX: Tired state   => OHIO

Not referring to weariness or sleepiness; this clue is about the U.S. state that manufactures lots of tires.

EX: Cock and bull   => MALES

The answer is not about nonsense or lying. "Cock" and "bull" are examples of the general plural "males". Note that "Rooster and stallion" could yield the same answer but would not be nearly as clever.

EX: First place   => EDEN (the garden)

EX: Present time   => YULE (or XMAS or NOEL)

EX: Inside shot   => XRAY

EX: Comes before fall   => PRIDE

EX: Insanity, at times   => PLEA

EX: It's often on the house   => LIEN

EX: Avoiding blows   => ALEE

CLUE APPRECIATION BONUS

Here's an example of a great clue that demonstrates many of the strategies included in this guide.

Nice time => **ETE**

AMBIGUOUS PRONUNCIATION: The clue word "Nice" is pronounced to rhyme with "peace" rather than with "rice", which would be the more obvious first choice.

PART OF SPEECH: At first glance, "Nice" looks like the adjective "pleasant" rather than a proper place name, the French city.

IMPLIED FOREIGN LANGUAGE: Since the clue refers to a city in France, it implies that the answer is a French word.

AMBIGUOUS CAPITAL LETTER: The first letter of every clue is a capital letter, masking the fact that the first word of this clue, being a place name, is actually always capitalized.

COMMON CROSSWORD ANSWERS: The word "ETE", meaning "summer" in French, appears very frequently in crossword puzzles. Its appeal is that it's a short, vowel-heavy word with easy-to-cross letters.

And **CLEVER MISDIRECTION**, because it's clever and misdirects you.

COMMON
CROSSWORD
ANSWERS

To fill a crossword grid, constructors often need to incorporate answers that are uncommon but have particularly useful letter combinations. They typically are short and heavy with vowels and easy crossing letters. These words, names, abbreviations, etc., belong on your **Crossword Crib Sheet**.

The capitalized entries below are some crossword repeaters. There are many more.

PEOPLE

Robert E. Lee (RELEE)	Confederate leader
Brian ENO	musician
ILIE Nastase, Arthur ASHE	tennis players
Ernie ELS	golfer
IDI AMIN	Uganda dictator
Mel OTT, the ALOUs	baseball players
Bobby ORR	hockey player
EERO Saarinen	architect
EDA LeShan	writer
ESAI Morales	actor
UMA Thurman	actress
ARTE Johnson	comedian
REM or ELO	rock bands
ELI	nickname for Yalie

PLACES

ODER, DEE, ISERE, AAR	rivers
ALTAI, URAL	mountains
ERIE, ADEN, ARAL	lakes, seas
EDEN	the Garden of...

FOREIGN WORDS

AMO, AMAS, AMAT	Latin forms of "to love"
ETE	French "summer"
ETAT	French "state"
NEE	French "born"
ECU, SOU	old French coins
EPEE	French fencing sword
ETRE, ESSE	"to be" in French, Latin
ADAR, ELUL	Hebrew months
UNO, DUO, TRE	Spanish numbers
TIA, NINO	Spanish relatives
NENE	Hawaiian goose
LEI	Hawaiian garland
CIAO	Italian "hello"

ACH	German exclamation

ABBREVIATIONS

NBAER or NLER	member of National Basketball Assn. or National League
RBI	runs batted in
ERA	earned run average or Equal Rights Amendment
TKO	technical knockout
EEE	Shoe width
AAA	Automobile Assn. of America or small battery
AMA, ADA, ABA	Amer. Medical, Dental, or Bar Assn.
IRA	Irish Republican Army or Individual Retirement Acct.
IRS	Internal Revenue Service
SSR	Soviet Socialist Republic
UAE	United Arab Emirates
YSL	Yves St. Laurent
RLS	Robert Louis Stevenson
TSE	T. S. Eliot
ETA, ETD	estimated time of arrival or departure

SST	supersonic transit
IOU	I owe you
SOS	HELP!
DDT	banned insecticide
TNT	explosive
SRO	standing room only
ASAP	as soon as possible

SOME ODD BUT COMMON USAGES

Compass directions, such as ESE or NNW

Roman numerals I, V, X, L, C, D, and M, are used in math, years, and hours on a clock (or sundial); the numbers 0 and 1 are used as letters O and I

Music

- Key of a particular musical piece INx, where x is the musical note A-G

- xFLAT, xMAJOR, where x is a musical note

- EIEIO, from "Old MacDonald Had a Farm"

- TRA (as in TRA-LA-LA)

- Plural of DO, RE, MI, etc.

Plurals of 2-letter abbreviations

- AMS, PMS – mornings, evenings

- ORS, ERS – operating, emergency rooms

- ETS – extra-terrestrials

- TDS - touchdowns

Letters on a telephone button or any other alphabetic sequence

Keys on a keyboard – TAB, ALT, CTRL, ESC

Text shorthand, like LOL, OMG, BTW, IMHO

Spelled out Greek letters, like ALPHA, BETA

TV station letters, like HBO, CBS

Airport codes like DCA, IAD, JFK, SFO, LAX, ORD

Playground retorts, like AMSO ("am so"), ISTOO ("is too")

GET TO WORK …AND HAVE FUN

You now have the foundation required to start solving any crossword puzzles, and to finish many of them. With practice, you'll be able to change that "many" to "most".

In summary:

- Make use of the tips.

- Trust your own knowledge of facts and your experience with the English language.

- Keep an open mind when analyzing each clue, thinking outside of the proverbial box.

- Learn something new and interesting along the way.

- Practice!

And remember that this is a game, so approach each crossword puzzle as an opportunity for fun and satisfaction.

Happy puzzling.